- **Exam Code:** N10-008
  Exam Title: CompTIA Network+
- **Exam Provider:** CompTIA

- **Exam Questions:** 200

QUESTION: 1

A systems administrator needs to improve WiFi performance in a densely populated office tower and use the latest standard. There is a mix of devices that use 2.4 GHz and 5 GHz. Which of the following should the systems administrator select to meet this requirement?

A. 802.11ac

B. 802.11ax

C. 802.11g

D. 802.11n

Answer(s): B

QUESTION: 2

Which of the following would be BEST to use to detect a MAC spoofing attack?

A. Internet Control Message Protocol

B. Reverse Address Resolution Protocol

C. Dynamic Host Configuration Protocol

D. Internet Message Access Protocol

Answer(s): B

QUESTION: 3

A technician receives feedback that some users are experiencing high amounts of jitter while using the wireless network. While troubleshooting the network, the technician uses the ping command with the IP address of the default gateway and verifies large variations in latency. The technician thinks the issue may be interference from other networks and non-802.11 devices. Which of the following tools should the technician use to troubleshoot the issue?

A. NetFlow analyzer

B. Bandwidth analyzer

C. Protocol analyzer

D. Spectrum analyzer

Answer(s): D

QUESTION: 4

Wireless users are reporting intermittent internet connectivity. Connectivity is restored when the users disconnect and reconnect, utilizing the web authentication process each time. The network administrator can see the devices connected to the APs at all times. Which of the following steps will MOST likely determine the cause of the issue?

A. Verify the session time-out configuration on the captive portal settings

B. Check for encryption protocol mismatch on the client's wireless settings

C. Confirm that a valid passphrase is being used during the web authentication

D. Investigate for a client's disassociation caused by an evil twin AP

Answer(s): A

QUESTION: 5

A network administrator walks into a datacenter and notices an unknown person is following closely. The administrator stops and directs the person to the security desk. Which of the following attacks did the network administrator prevent?

A. Evil twin

B. Tailgating

C. Piggybacking

D. Shoulder surfing

Answer(s): B

QUESTION: 6

A network administrator needs to provide remote clients with access to an internal web application. Which of the following methods provides the HIGHEST flexibility and compatibility while encrypting only the connection to the web application?

A. Clientless VPN

B. Virtual desktop

C. Virtual network computing

D. mGRE tunnel

Answer(s): A

QUESTION: 7

A network is experiencing a number of CRC errors during normal network communication. At which of the following layers of the OSI model will the administrator MOST likely start to troubleshoot?

A. Layer 1

B. Layer 2

C. Layer 3

D. Layer 4

E. Layer 5

F. Layer 6

G. Layer 7

Answer(s): B

QUESTION: 8

A client recently added 100 users who are using VMs. All users have since reported slow or unresponsive desktops. Reports show minimal network congestion, zero packet loss, and acceptable packet delay. Which of the following metrics will MOST accurately show the underlying performance issues? (Choose two.)

A. CPU usage

B. Memory

C. Temperature

D. Bandwidth

E. Latency

F. Jitter

Answer(s): A,B

QUESTION: 9

Client devices cannot enter a network, and the network administrator determines the DHCP scope is exhausted. The administrator wants to avoid creating a new DHCP pool. Which of the following can the administrator perform to resolve the issue?

A. Install load balancers

B. Install more switches

C. Decrease the number of VLANs

D. Reduce the lease time

Answer(s): D

QUESTION: 10

An administrator is writing a script to periodically log the IPv6 and MAC addresses of all the devices on a network segment. Which of the following switch features will MOST likely be used to assist with this task?

A. Spanning Tree Protocol

B. Neighbor Discovery Protocol

C. Link Aggregation Control Protocol

D. Address Resolution Protocol

Answer(s): B

QUESTION: 11

Which of the following DNS records works as an alias to another record?

A. AAAA

B. CNAME

C. MX

D. SOA

Answer(s): B

QUESTION: 12

A company built a new building at its headquarters location. The new building is connected to the company's LAN via fiber-optic cable. Multiple users in the new building are unable to access the company's intranet site via their web browser, but they are able to access internet sites. Which of the following describes how the network administrator can resolve this issue?

A. Correct the DNS server entries in the DHCP scope

B. Correct the external firewall gateway address

C. Correct the NTP server settings on the clients

D. Correct a TFTP Issue on the company's server

Answer(s): A

QUESTION: 13

A technician is installing a new fiber connection to a network device in a datacenter. The connection from the device to the switch also traverses a patch panel connection. The chain of connections is in the following   order:

-Device
-LC/LC   patch   cable
-Patch   panel

-Cross-connect   fiber   cable
-Patch   panel
-LC/LC   patch   cable
-Switch

The connection is not working. The technician has changed both patch cables with known working patch cables. The device had been tested and was working properly before being installed. Which of the following is the MOST likely cause of the issue?

A. TX/RX is reversed

B. An incorrect cable was used

C. The device failed during installation

D. Attenuation is occurring

Answer(s): A

QUESTION: 14

A technician is searching for a device that is connected to the network and has the device's physical network address. Which of the following should the technician review on the switch to locate the device's network port?

A. IP route table

B. VLAN tag

C. MAC table

D. QoS tag

Answer(s): C

QUESTION: 15

Which of the following provides redundancy on a file server to ensure the server is still connected to a LAN even in the event of a port failure on a switch?

A. NIC teaming

B. Load balancer

C. RAID array

D. PDUs

Answer(s): A

QUESTION: 16

An IT organization needs to optimize speeds for global content distribution and wants to reduce latency in high-density user locations. Which of the following technologies BEST meets the organization's requirements?

A. Load balancing

B. Geofencing

C. Public cloud

D. Content delivery network

E. Infrastructure as a service

Answer(s): D

QUESTION: 17

A user reports being unable to access network resources after making some changes in the office. Which of the following should a network technician do FIRST?

A. Check the system's IP address

B. Do a ping test against the servers

C. Reseat the cables into the back of the PC

D. Ask what changes were made

Answer(s): D

QUESTION: 18

A new cabling certification is being requested every time a network technician rebuilds one end of a Cat 6 (vendor-certified) cable to create a crossover connection that is used to connect switches. Which of the following would address this issue by allowing the use of the original cable?

A. CSMA/CD

B. LACP

C. PoE+

D. MDIX

Answer(s): D

QUESTION: 19

A company hired a technician to find all the devices connected within a network. Which of the following software tools would BEST assist the technician in completing this task?

A. IP scanner

B. Terminal emulator

C. NetFlow analyzer

D. Port scanner

Answer(s): A

QUESTION: 20

A technician is installing a high-density wireless network and wants to use an available frequency that supports the maximum number of channels to reduce interference. Which of the following standard 802.11 frequency ranges should the technician look for while reviewing WAP specifications?

A. 2.4GHz

B. 5GHz

C. 6GHz

D. 900MHz

Answer(s): B

QUESTION: 21

A technician is configuring a network switch to be used in a publicly accessible location. Which of the following should the technician configure on the switch to prevent unintended connections?

A. DHCP snooping

B. Geofencing

C. Port security

D. Secure SNMP

Answer(s): C

QUESTION: 22

Which of the following is used to track and document various types of known vulnerabilities?

A. CVE

B. Penetration testing

C. Zero-day

D. SIEM

E. Least privilege

Answer(s): A

QUESTION: 23

The network administrator is informed that a user's email password is frequently hacked by brute-force programs. Which of the following policies should the network administrator implements to BEST mitigate this issue? (Choose two.)

A. Captive portal

B. Two-factor authentication

C. Complex passwords

D. Geofencing

E. Role-based access

F. Explicit deny

Answer(s): B,C

QUESTION: 24

A network engineer performs the following tasks to increase server bandwidth:

-Connects two network cables from the server to a switch stack
-Configure   LACP   on   the   switchports
-Verifies the correct configurations on the switch interfaces

Which of the following needs to be configured on the server?

A. Load balancing

B. Multipathing

C. NIC teaming

D. Clustering

Answer(s): C

QUESTION: 25

A network technician is manually configuring the network settings for a new device and is told the network block is 192.168.0.0/20. Which of the following subnets should the technician use?

A. 255.255.128.0

B. 255.255.192.0

C. 255.255.240.0

D. 255.255.248.0

Answer(s): C

QUESTION: 26

Which of the following is the LARGEST MTU for a standard Ethernet frame?

A. 1452

B. 1492

C. 1500

D. 2304

Answer(s): C

QUESTION: 27

Given   the   following   information:

Protocol	Local address	Foreign address	State
TCP	127.0.0.1:57779	Desktop-Open:57780	Established
TCP	127.0.0.1:57780	Desktop-Open:57779	Established

Which of the following command-line tools would generate this output?

A. netstat

B. arp

C. dig

D. tracert

Answer(s): A

QUESTION: 28

According to troubleshooting methodology, which of the following should the technician do NEXT after determining the most likely probable cause of an issue?

A. Establish a plan of action to resolve the issue and identify potential effects

B. Verify full system functionality and, if applicable, implement preventive measures

C. Implement the solution or escalate as necessary

D. Test the theory to determine the cause

Answer(s): D

QUESTION: 29

Which of the following BEST describes a network appliance that warns of unapproved devices that are accessing the network?

A. Firewall

B. AP

C. Proxy server

D. IDS

Answer(s): D

QUESTION: 30

A technician is installing a cable modem in a SOHO. Which of the following cable types will the technician MOST likely use to connect a modem to the ISP?

A. Coaxial

B. Single-mode fiber

C. Cat 6e

D. Multimode fiber

Answer(s): A

QUESTION: 31

A network technician is reviewing the interface counters on a router interface. The technician is attempting to confirm a cable issue. Given the following information:

Metric	Value
Last cleared	7 minutes, 34 seconds
# of packets output	6915
# of packets input	270
CRCs	183
Giants	0
Runts	0
Multicasts	14

Which of the following metrics confirms there is a cabling issue?

A. Last cleared

B. Number of packets output

C. CRCs

D. Giants

E. Multicasts

Answer(s): C

QUESTION: 32

Which of the following is the physical topology for an Ethernet LAN?

A. Bus

B. Ring

C. Mesh

D. Star

Answer(s): D

QUESTION: 33

An IT director is setting up new disaster and HA policies for a company. Limited downtime is critical to operations. To meet corporate requirements, the director set up two different datacenters across the country that will stay current on data and applications. In the event of an outage, the company can immediately switch from one datacenter to another. Which of the following does this BEST describe?

A. A warm site

B. Data mirroring

C. Multipathing

D. Load balancing

E. A hot site

Answer(s): E

QUESTION: 34

The management team needs to ensure unnecessary modifications to the corporate network are not permitted and version control is maintained. Which of the following documents would BEST support this?

A. An incident response plan

B. A business continuity plan

C. A change management policy

D. An acceptable use policy

Answer(s): C

QUESTION: 35

Which of the following is MOST likely to generate significant East-West traffic in a datacenter?

    A. A backup of a large video presentation to cloud storage for archival purposes

    B. A duplication of a hosted virtual server to another physical server for redundancy

    C. A download of navigation data to a portable device for offline access

    D. A query from an IoT device to a cloud-hosted server for a firmware update

Answer(s): B

QUESTION: 36

A technician is troubleshooting a network switch that seems to stop responding to requests intermittently whenever the logging level is set for debugging. Which of the following metrics should the technician check to begin troubleshooting the issue?

A. Audit logs

B. CPU utilization

C. CRC errors

D. Jitter

Answer(s): B

QUESTION: 37

A technician wants to deploy a new wireless network that comprises 30 WAPs installed throughout a three-story office building. All the APs will broadcast the same SSID for client access. Which of the following BEST describes this deployment?

A. Extended service set

B. Basic service set

C. Unified service set

D. Independent basic service set

Answer(s): A

QUESTION: 38

A user tries to ping 192.168.1.100 from the command prompt on the 192.168.2.101 network but gets the following response: U.U.U.U. Which of the following needs to be configured for these networks to reach each other?

A. Network address translation

B. Default gateway

C. Loopback

D. Routing protocol

Answer(s): B

QUESTION: 39

A branch of a company recently switched to a new ISP. The network engineer was given a new IP range to assign. The ISP assigned 196.26.4.0/26, and the branch gateway router now has the following configurations on the interface that peers to the ISP:

```
IP address:      196.26.4.30
Subnet mask:     255.255.255.224
Gateway:         196.24.4.1
```

The network engineer observes that all users have lost Internet connectivity. Which of the following describes the issue?

A. The incorrect subnet mask was configured

B. The incorrect gateway was configured

C. The incorrect IP address was configured

D. The incorrect interface was configured

Answer(s): A

QUESTION: 40

Within the realm of network security, Zero Trust:

A. prevents attackers from moving laterally through a system.

B. allows a server to communicate with outside networks without a firewall.

C. block malicious software that is too new to be found in virus definitions.

D. stops infected files from being downloaded via websites.

Answer(s): A

QUESTION: 41

Which of the following service models would MOST likely be used to replace on-premises servers with a cloud solution?

A. PaaS

B. IaaS

C. SaaS

D. Disaster recovery as a Service (DRaaS)

Answer(s): B

QUESTION: 42

Which of the following factors should be considered when evaluating a firewall to protect a datacenter's east-west traffic?

A. Replication traffic between an on-premises server and a remote backup facility

B. Traffic between VMs running on different hosts

C. Concurrent connections generated by Internet DDoS attacks

D. VPN traffic from remote offices to the datacenter's VMs

Answer(s): A

QUESTION: 43

SIMULATION
You are tasked with verifying the following requirements are met in order to ensure network security.

Requirements:

Datacenter

-Ensure network is subnetted to allow all devices to communicate properly while minimizing address space usage
-Provide a dedicated server to resolve IP addresses and hostnames correctly and handle port 53 traffic Building A
-Ensure network is subnetted to allow all devices to communicate properly while minimizing address space usage
-Provide devices to support 5 additional different office users
-Add an additional mobile user
-Replace the Telnet server with a more secure solution Screened subnet
-Ensure network is subnetted to allow all devices to communicate properly while minimizing address space usage
-Provide a server to handle external 80/443 traffic
-Provide a server to handle port 20/21 traffic

INSTRUCTIONS

Drag and drop objects onto the appropriate locations. Objects can be used multiple times and not all placeholders need to be filled. Available objects are located in both the Servers and Devices tabs of the Drag & Drop menu.

If at any time you would like to bring back the initial state of the simulation, please click the Reset All button.

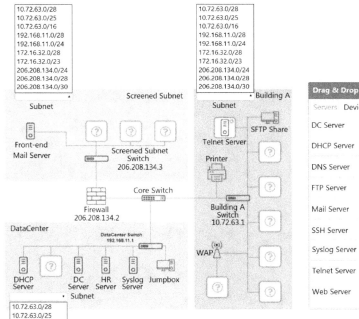

10.72.63.0/28
10.72.63.0/25
10.72.63.0/16
192.168.11.0/28
192.168.11.0/24
172.16.32.0/28
172.16.32.0/23
206.208.134.0/24
206.208.134.0/28
206.208.134.0/30

Screened Subnet

Subnet

Front-end
Mail Server

Screened Subnet
Switch
206.208.134.3

Core Switch

Firewall
206.208.134.2

DataCenter

DataCenter Switch
192.168.11.1

DHCP
Server

DC
Server

HR
Server

Syslog
Server

Jumpbox

• Subnet

10.72.63.0/28
10.72.63.0/25
10.72.63.0/16
192.168.11.0/28
192.168.11.0/24
172.16.32.0/28
172.16.32.0/23
206.208.134.0/24
206.208.134.0/28
206.208.134.0/30

10.72.63.0/28
10.72.63.0/25
10.72.63.0/16
192.168.11.0/28
192.168.11.0/24
172.16.32.0/28
172.16.32.0/23
206.208.134.0/24
206.208.134.0/28
206.208.134.0/30

• Building A

Subnet

SFTP Share

Telnet Server

Printer

Building A
Switch
10.72.63.1

WAP

Drag & Drop

Servers   Devices

DC Server

DHCP Server

DNS Server

FTP Server

Mail Server

SSH Server

Syslog Server

Telnet Server

Web Server

Drag & Drop

Servers   Devices

Jumpbox

Laptop

Printer

SFTP Share

WAP

Workstation

A. See Explanation section for answer.

Answer(s): A

Explanation:
Top left subnet – 206.208.134.0/28
Top right subnet – 10.72.63.0/28
Bottom subnet – 192.168.11.0/28

Screened Subnet devices – Web server, FTP server
Building A devices – SSH server top left, workstations on all 5 on the right, laptop on bottom left DataCenter devices – DNS server.

QUESTION: 44

Which of the following is used to prioritize Internet usage per application and per user on the network?

A. Bandwidth management

B. Load balance routing

C. Border Gateway Protocol

D. Administrative distance

Answer(s): A

QUESTION: 45

A network administrator needs to query the NSs for a remote application. Which of the following commands would BEST help the administrator accomplish this task?

A. dig

B. arp

C. showinterface

D. hostname

Answer(s): A

QUESTION: 46

Which of the following would MOST likely be used to review previous upgrades to a system?

A. Business continuity plan

B. Change management

C. System life cycle

D. Standard operating procedures

Answer(s): B

A technician is deploying a new switch model and would like to add it to the existing network monitoring software. The technician wants to know what metrics can be gathered from a given switch. Which of the following should the technician utilize for the switch?

A. MIB

B. Trap

C. Syslog

D. Audit log

Answer(s): A

A network device is configured to send critical events to a syslog server; however, the following alerts are not being received:

Severity 5 LINK-UPDOWN: Interface 1/1, changed state to down
Severity 5 LINK-UPDOWN: Interface 1/3, changed state to down

Which of the following describes the reason why the events are not being received?

A. The network device is not configured to log that level to the syslog server

B. The network device was down and could not send the event

C. The syslog server is not compatible with the network device

D. The syslog server did not have the correct MIB loaded to receive the message

Answer(s): A

QUESTION: 49

A network administrator is implementing OSPF on all of a company's network devices. Which of the following will MOST likely replace all the company's hubs?

A. A Layer 3 switch

B. A proxy server

C. A NGFW

D. A WLAN controller

Answer(s): A

QUESTION: 50

A network administrator discovers that users in an adjacent building are connecting to the company's guest wireless network to download inappropriate material. Which of the following can the administrator do to MOST easily mitigate this issue?

A. Reduce the wireless power levels

B. Adjust the wireless channels

C. Enable wireless client isolation

D. Enable wireless port security

Answer(s): A

QUESTION: 51

A network administrator is designing a new datacenter in a different region that will need to communicate to the old datacenter with a secure connection. Which of the following access methods would provide the BEST security for this new datacenter?

A. Virtual network computing

B. Secure Socket Shell

C. In-band connection

D. Site-to-site VPN

Answer(s): D

QUESTION: 52

An attacker is attempting to find the password to a network by inputting common words and phrases in plaintext to the password prompt. Which of the following attack types BEST describes this action?

A. Pass-the-hash attack

B. Rainbow table attack

C. Brute-force attack

D. Dictionary attack

Answer(s): D

QUESTION: 53

Which of the following technologies provides a failover mechanism for the default gateway?

A. FHRP

B. LACP

C. OSPF

D. STP

Answer(s): A

QUESTION: 54

The following configuration is applied to a DHCP server connected to a   VPN   concentrator:

IP address: 10.0.0.1
Subnet mask: 255.255.255.0
Gateway: 10.0.0.254

There are 300 non-concurrent sales representatives who log in for one hour a day to upload reports, and 252 of these representatives are able to connect to the VPN without any Issues. The remaining sales representatives cannot connect to the VPN over the course of the day. Which of the following can be done to resolve the issue without utilizing additional resources?

A. Decrease the lease duration

B. Reboot the DHCP server

C. Install a new VPN concentrator

D. Configure a new router

Answer(s): A

QUESTION: 55

A technician needs to configure a Linux computer for network monitoring. The technician has the following information: Linux computer   details:

Interface	IP address	MAC address
eth0	10.1.2.24	A1:B2:C3:F4:E5:D6

Switch   mirror   port   details:

Interface	IP address	MAC address
eth1	10.1.2.3	A1:B2:C3:D4:E5:F6

After connecting the Linux computer to the mirror port on the switch, which of the following commands should the technician run on the Linux computer?

A. ifconfig ecth0 promisc

B. ifconfig eth1 up

C. ifconfig eth0 10.1.2.3

D. ifconfig eth1 hw ether A1:B2:C3:D4:E5:F6

Answer(s): A

QUESTION: 56

A network engineer is investigating reports of poor network performance. Upon reviewing a device configuration, the engineer finds that duplex settings are mismatched on both ends. Which of the following would be the MOST likely result of this finding?

A. Increased CRC errors

B. Increased giants and runts

C. Increased switching loops

D. Increased device temperature

Answer(s): A

QUESTION: 57

Which of the following devices would be used to manage a corporate WLAN?

A. A wireless NAS

B. A wireless bridge

C. A wireless router

D. A wireless controller

Answer(s): D

QUESTION: 58

Which of the following types of devices can provide content filtering and threat protection, and manage multiple IPSec site-to-site connections?

A. Layer 3 switch

B. VPN headend

C. Next-generation firewall

D. Proxy server

E. Intrusion prevention

Answer(s): C

QUESTION: 59

An engineer notices some late collisions on a half-duplex link. The engineer verifies that the devices on both ends of the connection are configured for half duplex. Which of the following is the MOST likely cause of this issue?

A. The link is improperly terminated

B. One of the devices is misconfigured

C. The cable length is excessive

D. One of the devices has a hardware issue

Answer(s): C

QUESTION: 60

A network administrator is configuring a load balancer for two systems. Which of the following must the administrator configure to ensure connectivity during a failover?

A. VIP

B. NAT

C. APIPA

D. IPv6 tunneling

E. Broadcast IP

Answer(s): A

QUESTION: 61

A technician is troubleshooting a wireless connectivity issue in a small office located in a high-rise building. Several APs are mounted in this office. The users report that the network connections frequently disconnect and reconnect throughout the day. Which of the following is the MOST likely cause of this issue?

A. The AP association time is set too low

B. EIRP needs to be boosted

C. Channel overlap is occurring

D. The RSSI is misreported

Answer(s): B

QUESTION: 62

A network engineer configured new firewalls with the correct configuration to be deployed to each remote branch. Unneeded services were disabled, and all firewall rules were applied successfully. Which of the following should the network engineer perform NEXT to ensure all the firewalls are hardened successfully?

   A. Ensure an implicit permit rule is enabled

   B. Configure the log settings on the firewalls to the central syslog server

   C. Update the firewalls with current firmware and software

   D. Use the same complex passwords on all firewalls

Answer(s): C

QUESTION: 63

At which of the following OSI model layers would a technician find an IP header?

   A. Layer 1

   B. Layer 2

   C. Layer 3

D. Layer 4

Answer(s): C

An engineer is configuring redundant network links between switches. Which of the following should the engineer enable to prevent network stability issues?

A. 802.1Q

B. STP

C. Flow control

D. CSMA/CD

Answer(s): B

Several WIFI users are reporting the inability to connect to the network. WLAN users on the guest network are able to access all network resources without any performance issues. The following table summarizes the findings after a site survey of the area in question:

Location	AP 1	AP 2	AP 3	AP 4
SSID	Corp1	Corp1	Corp1/Guest	Corp1/Guest
Channel	2	1	5	11
RSSI	-81dBm	-82dBm	-44dBm	-41dBm
Antenna type	Omni	Omni	Directional	Directional

Which of the following should a wireless technician do NEXT to troubleshoot this issue?

A. Reconfigure the channels to reduce overlap

B. Replace the omni antennas with directional antennas

C. Update the SSIDs on all the APs

D. Decrease power in AP 3 and AP 4

Answer(s): A

QUESTION: 66

Which of the following routing protocols is used to exchange route information between public autonomous systems?

A. OSPF

B. BGP

C. EGRIP

D. RIP

Answer(s): B

A fiber link connecting two campus networks is broken. Which of the following tools should an engineer use to detect the exact break point of the fiber link?

A. OTDR

B. Tone generator

C. Fusion splicer

D. Cable tester

E. PoE injector

Answer(s): A

Which of the following can be used to centrally manage credentials for various types of administrative privileges on configured network devices?

A. SSO

B. TACACS+

C. Zero Trust

D. Separation of duties

E. Multifactor authentication

Answer(s): B

QUESTION: 69

A network technician is installing new software on a Windows-based server in a different geographical location. Which of the following would be BEST for the technician to use to perform this task?

A. RDP

B. SSH

C. FTP

D. DNS

Answer(s): A

QUESTION: 70

Branch users are experiencing issues with videoconferencing. Which of the following will the company MOST likely configure to improve performance for these applications?

   A. Link Aggregation Control Protocol

   B. Dynamic routing

   C. Quality of service

   D. Network load balancer

   E. Static IP addresses

Answer(s): C

QUESTION: 71

A technician is assisting a user who cannot connect to a network resource. The technician first checks for a link light. According to troubleshooting methodology, this is an example of:

A. using a bottom-to-top approach.

B. establishing a plan of action.

C. documenting a finding.

D. questioning the obvious.

Answer(s): D

QUESTION: 72

Which of the following transceiver types can support up to 40Gbps?

A. SFP+

B. QSFP+

C. QSFP

D. SFP

Answer(s): B

QUESTION: 73

Which of the following TCP ports is used by the Windows OS for file sharing?

A. 53

B. 389

C. 445

D. 1433

Answer(s): C

QUESTION: 74

A network administrator redesigned the positioning of the APs to create adjacent areas of wireless coverage. After project validation, some users still report poor connectivity when their devices maintain an association to a distanced AP. Which of the following should the network administrator check FIRST?

A. Validate the roaming settings on the APs and WLAN clients

B. Verify that the AP antenna type is correct for the new layout

C. Check to see if MU-MIMO was properly activated on the APs

D. Deactivate the 2.4GHz band on the APS

Answer(s): A

QUESTION: 75

Which of the following connector types would have the MOST flexibility?

A. SFP

B. BNC

C. LC

D. RJ45

Answer(s): A

QUESTION: 76

Which of the following ports is commonly used by VoIP phones?

A. 20

B. 143

C. 445

D. 5060

Answer(s): D

A network engineer is investigating reports of poor network performance. Upon reviewing a report, the engineer finds that jitter at the office is greater than 10ms on the only WAN connection available. Which of the following would be MOST affected by this statistic?

A. A VoIP sales call with a customer

B. An in-office video call with a coworker

C. Routing table from the ISP

D. Firewall CPU processing time

Answer(s): A

QUESTION: 78

A network technician needs to ensure outside users are unable to telnet into any of the servers at the datacenter. Which of the following ports should be blocked when checking firewall configuration?

A. 22

B. 23

C. 80

D. 3389

E. 8080

Answer(s): B

QUESTION: 79

A technician is writing documentation regarding a company's server farm. The technician needs to confirm the server name for all Linux servers. Which of the following commands should the technician run?

A. ipconfig

B. nslookup

C. arp

D. route

Answer(s): B

QUESTION: 80

A technician is connecting multiple switches to create a large network for a new office. The switches are unmanaged Layer 2 switches with multiple connections between each pair. The network is experiencing an extreme amount of latency. Which of the following is MOST likely occurring?

A. Ethernet collisions

B. A DDoS attack

C. A broadcast storm

D. Routing loops

Answer(s): C

QUESTION: 81

A store owner would like to have secure wireless access available for both business equipment and patron use. Which of the following features should be configured to allow different wireless access through the same equipment?

A. MIMO

B. TKIP

C. LTE

D. SSID

Answer(s): D

QUESTION: 82

Which of the following systems would MOST likely be found in a screened subnet?

A. RADIUS

B. FTP

C. SQL

D. LDAP

Answer(s): B

QUESTION: 83

Which of the following would need to be configured to ensure a device with a specific MAC address is always assigned the same IP address from DHCP?

A. Scope options

B. Reservation

C. Dynamic assignment

D. Exclusion

E. Static assignment

Answer(s): B

QUESTION: 84

Access to a datacenter should be individually recorded by a card reader even when multiple employees enter the facility at the same time. Which of the following allows the enforcement of this policy?

A. Motion detection

B. Access control vestibules

C. Smart lockers

D. Cameras

Answer(s): B

QUESTION: 85

A workstation is configured with the following network details:

IP address	Subnet mask	Default gateway
10.1.2.23	10.1.2.0/27	10.1.2.1

Software on the workstation needs to send a query to the local subnet broadcast address. To which of the following addresses should the software be configured to send the query?

A. 10.1.2.0

B. 10.1.2.1

C. 10.1.2.23

D. 10.1.2.255

E. 10.1.2.31

Answer(s): E

QUESTION: 86

After the A record of a public website was updated, some visitors were unable to access the website. Which of the following should be adjusted to address the issue?

A. TTL

B. MX

C. TXT

D. SOA

Answer(s): A

QUESTION: 87

A network administrator is installing a wireless network at a client's office. Which of the following IEEE 802.11 standards would be BEST to use for multiple simultaneous client access?

A. CDMA

B. CSMA/CD

C. CSMA/CA

D. GSM

Answer(s): C

QUESTION: 88

A technician is installing multiple UPS units in a major retail store. The technician is required to keep track of all changes to new and old equipment. Which of the following will allow the technician to record these changes?

A. Asset tags

B. A smart locker

C. An access control vestibule

D. A camera

Answer(s): A

QUESTION: 89

Which of the following attacks encrypts user data and requires a proper backup implementation to recover?

A. DDoS

B. Phishing

C. Ransomware

D. MAC spoofing

Answer(s): C

QUESTION: 90

A network administrator wants to analyze attacks directed toward the company's network. Which of the following must the network administrator implement to assist in this goal?

A. A honeypot

B. Network segmentation

C. Antivirus

D. A screened subnet

Answer(s): A

QUESTION: 91

A network administrator is configuring a database server and would like to ensure the database engine is listening on a certain port. Which of the following commands should the administrator use to accomplish this goal?

A. nslookup

B. netstat -a

C. ipconfig /a

D. arp -a

Answer(s): B

QUESTION: 92

A technician is implementing a new wireless network to serve guests at a local office. The network needs to provide Internet access but disallow associated stations from communicating with each other. Which of the following would BEST accomplish this requirement?

A. Wireless client isolation

B. Port security

C. Device geofencing

D. DHCP snooping

Answer(s): A

QUESTION: 93

A company requires a disaster recovery site to have equipment ready to go in the event of a disaster at its main datacenter. The company does not have the budget to mirror all the live data to the disaster recovery site. Which of the following concepts should the company select?

A. Cold site

B. Hot site

C. Warm site

D. Cloud site

Answer(s): C

QUESTION: 94

An IT technician suspects a break in one of the uplinks that provides connectivity to the core switch. Which of the following command-line tools should the technician use to determine where the incident is occurring?

A. nslookup

B. show config

C. netstat

D. show interface

E. show counters

Answer(s): D

A technician is connecting DSL for a new customer. After installing and connecting the on-premises equipment, the technician verifies DSL synchronization. When connecting to a workstation, however, the link LEDs on the workstation and modem do not light up. Which of the following should the technician perform during troubleshooting?

A. Identify the switching loops between the modem and the workstation.

B. Check for asymmetrical routing on the modem.

C. Look for a rogue DHCP server on the network.

D. Replace the cable connecting the modem and the workstation.

Answer(s): D

Which of the following services can provide data storage, hardware options, and scalability to a third-party company that cannot afford new devices?

A. SaaS

B. IaaS

C. PaaS

D. DaaS

Answer(s): B

QUESTION: 97

A network administrator is talking to different vendors about acquiring technology to support a new project for a large company. Which of the following documents will MOST likely need to be signed before information about the project is shared?

A. BYOD policy

B. NDA

C. SLA

D. MOU

Answer(s): B

Two remote offices need to be connected securely over an untrustworthy MAN. Each office needs to access network shares at the other site. Which of the following will BEST provide this functionality?

A. Client-to-site VPN

B. Third-party VPN service

C. Site-to-site VPN

D. Split-tunnel VPN

Answer(s): C

A network requirement calls for segmenting departments into different networks. The campus network is set up with users of each department in multiple buildings. Which of the following should be configured to keep the design simple and efficient?

A. MDIX

B. Jumbo frames

C. Port tagging

D. Flow control

Answer(s): C

Which of the following protocols will a security appliance that is correlating network events from multiple devices MOST likely rely on to receive event messages?

A. Syslog

B. Session Initiation Protocol

C. Secure File Transfer Protocol

D. Server Message Block

Answer(s): A

Which of the following is MOST commonly used to address CVEs on network equipment and/or operating systems?

A. Vulnerability assessment

B. Factory reset

C. Firmware update

D. Screened subnet

Answer(s): C

QUESTION: 102

A network technician is investigating an issue with handheld devices in a warehouse. Devices have not been connecting to the nearest APs, but they have been connecting to an AP on the far side of the warehouse.
Which of the following is the MOST likely cause of this issue?

A. The nearest APs are configured for 802.11g.

B. An incorrect channel assignment is on the nearest APs.

C. The power level is too high for the AP on the far side.

D. Interference exists around the AP on the far side.

Answer(s): C

Which of the following uses the destination IP address to forward packets?

A. A bridge

B. A Layer 2 switch

C. A router

D. A repeater

Answer(s): C

Which of the following OSI model layers is where conversations between applications are established, coordinated, and terminated?

A. Session

B. Physical

C. Presentation

D. Data link

Answer(s): A

QUESTION: 105

A business is using the local cable company to provide Internet access. Which of the following types of cabling will the cable company MOST likely use from the demarcation point back to the central office?

A. Multimode

B. Cat 5e

C. RG-6

D. Cat 6

E. 100BASE-T

Answer(s): C

QUESTION: 106

A network administrator decided to use SLAAC in an extensive IPv6 deployment to alleviate IP address management. The devices were properly connected into the LAN but autoconfiguration of the IP address did not occur as expected. Which of the following should the network administrator verify?

A. The network gateway is configured to send router advertisements.

B. A DHCP server is present on the same broadcast domain as the clients.

C. The devices support dual stack on the network layer.

D. The local gateway supports anycast routing.

Answer(s): A

QUESTION: 107

Which of the following is used to provide networking capability for VMs at Layer 2 of the OSI model?

A. VPN

B. VRRP

C. vSwitch

D. VIP

Answer(s): C

QUESTION: 108

A network administrator is required to ensure that auditors have read-only access to the system logs, while systems administrators have read and write access to the system logs, and operators have no access to the system logs. The network administrator has configured security groups for each of these functional categories. Which of the following security capabilities will allow the network administrator to maintain these permissions with the LEAST administrative effort?

A. Mandatory access control

B. User-based permissions

C. Role-based access

D. Least privilege

Answer(s): C

QUESTION: 109

Which of the following would be used to expedite MX record updates to authoritative NSs?

A. UDP forwarding

B. DNS caching

C. Recursive lookup

D. Time to live

Answer(s): D

QUESTION: 110

A client moving into a new office wants the IP network set up to accommodate 412 network-connected devices that are all on the same subnet. The subnet needs to be as small as possible. Which of the following subnet masks should be used to achieve the required result?

A. 255.255.0.0

B. 255.255.252.0

C. 255.255.254.0

D. 255.255.255.0

Answer(s): C

QUESTION: 111

A company is being acquired by a large corporation. As part of the acquisition process, the company's address should now redirect clients to the corporate organization page. Which of the following DNS records needs to be created?

A. SOA

B. NS

C. CNAME

D. TXT

Answer(s): C

Reference:
https://www.namecheap.com/support/knowledgebase/article.aspx/9604/2237/types-of-domainredirects-301-302-url-redirects-url-frame-and-cname/#:~:text=CNAME%20record%20is%20actually%20not,often%20mistakenly%20used%20as%20such.&text=In%20other%20words%2C%20CNAME%20record,address%20of%20the%20destination%20hostname

QUESTION: 112

A user is having difficulty with video conferencing and is looking for assistance. Which of the following would BEST improve performance?

A. Packet shaping

B. Quality of service

C. Port mirroring

D. Load balancing

Answer(s): B

QUESTION: 113

A network technician is configuring a new firewall for a company with the necessary access requirements to be allowed through the firewall. Which of the following would normally be applied as the LAST rule in the firewall?

A. Secure SNMP

B. Port security

C. Implicit deny

D. DHCP snooping

Answer(s): C

QUESTION: 114

A technician wants to install a WAP in the center of a room that provides service in a radius surrounding a radio. Which of the following antenna types should the AP utilize?

A. Omni

B. Directional

C. Yagi

D. Parabolic

Answer(s): A

QUESTION: 115

A systems administrator is running a VoIP network and is experiencing jitter and high latency. Which of the following would BEST help the administrator determine the cause of these issues?

A. Enabling RADIUS on the network

B. Configuring SNMP traps on the network

C. Implementing LDAP on the network

D. Establishing NTP on the network

Answer(s): B

QUESTION: 116

The following instructions were published about the proper network configuration for a videoconferencing device: "Configure a valid static RFC1918 address for your network. Check the option to use a connection over NAT." Which of the following is a valid IP address configuration for the device?

A. FE80::1

B. 100.64.0.1

C. 169.254.1.2

D. 172.19.0.2

E. 224.0.0.12

Answer(s): D

QUESTION: 117

A network administrator is reviewing interface errors on a switch. Which of the following indicates that a switchport is receiving packets in excess of the configured MTU?

A. CRC errors

B. Giants

C. Runts

D. Flooding

Answer(s): B

QUESTION: 118

A network administrator needs to implement an HDMI over IP solution. Which of the following will the networkadministrator MOST likely use to ensure smooth video delivery?

A. Link aggregation control

B. Port tagging

C. Jumbo frames

D. Media access control

Answer(s): C

A network administrator wants to reduce overhead and increase efficiency on a SAN. Which of the following can be configured to achieve these goals?

A. Port aggregation

B. Traffic shaping

C. Jumbo frames

D. Flow control

Answer(s): C

A rogue AP was found plugged in and providing Internet access to employees in the break room. Which of the following would be BEST to use to stop this from happening without physically removing the WAP?

A. Password complexity

B. Port security

C. Wireless client isolation

D. Secure SNMP

Answer(s): B

QUESTION: 121

A company's network is set up so all Internet-bound traffic from all remote offices exits through a main datacenter. Which of the following network topologies would BEST describe this setup?

A. Bus

B. Spine-and-leaf

C. Hub-and-spoke

D. Mesh

Answer(s): C

QUESTION: 122

To comply with industry requirements, a security assessment on the cloud server should identify which protocols and weaknesses are being exposed to attackers on the Internet. Which of the following tools is the MOST appropriate to complete the assessment?

A. Use tcpdump and parse the output file in a protocol analyzer.

B. Use an IP scanner and target the cloud WAN network addressing.

C. Run netstat in each cloud server and retrieve the running processes.

D. Use nmap and set the servers' public IPs as the targets.

Answer(s): D

QUESTION: 123

A systems administrator is configuring a firewall using NAT with PAT. Which of the following would be BEST suited for the LAN interface?

A. 172.15.0.0/18

B. 172.18.0.0/10

C. 172.23.0.0/16

D. 172.28.0.0/8

E. 172.32.0.0/14

Answer(s): C

QUESTION: 124

A packet is assigned a value to ensure it does not traverse a network indefinitely. Which of the following BEST represents this value?

A. Zero Trust

B. Planned obsolescence

C. Time to live

D. Caching

Answer(s): C

QUESTION: 125

Which of the following policies should be referenced when a user wants to access work email on a personal cell phone?

A. Offboarding policy

B. Acceptable use policy

C. BYOD policy

D. Remote access policy

Answer(s): C

QUESTION: 126

After a firewall replacement, some alarms and metrics related to network availability stopped updating on a monitoring system relying on SNMP. Which of the following should the network administrator do FIRST?

A. Modify the device's MIB on the monitoring system.

B. Configure syslog to send events to the monitoring system.

C. Use port mirroring to redirect traffic to the monitoring system.

D. Deploy SMB to transfer data to the monitoring system.

Answer(s): A

QUESTION: 127

At the destination host, which of the following OSI model layers will discard a segment with a bad checksum in the UDP header?

A. Network

B. Data link

C. Transport

D. Session

Answer(s): C

A voice engineer is troubleshooting a phone issue. When a call is placed, the caller hears echoes of the receiver's voice. Which of the following are the causes of this issue? (Choose two.)

A. Jitter

B. Speed mismatch

C. QoS misconfiguration

D. Protocol mismatch

E. CRC errors

F. Encapsulation errors

Answer(s): A,C

QUESTION: 129

Which of the following VPN configurations should be used to separate Internet and corporate traffic?

A. Split-tunnel

B. Remote desktop gateway

C. Site-to-site

D. Out-of-band management

Answer(s): A

QUESTION: 130

Which of the following is required when connecting an endpoint device with an RJ45 port to a network device with an ST port?

A. A media converter

B. A bridge

C. An MDIX

D. A load balancer

Answer(s): A

QUESTION: 131

The management team has instituted a 48-hour RTO as part of the disaster recovery plan. Which of the following procedures would meet the policy's requirements?

A. Recover all systems to a loss of 48 hours of data.

B. Limit network downtime to a maximum of 48 hours per year.

C. Recover all systems within 48 hours.

D. Require 48 hours of system backup maintenance.

Answer(s): C

Reference:
https://www.druva.com/blog/understanding-rpo-and-rto/

QUESTION: 132

Which of the following cable types would MOST likely be used to provide high-speed network connectivity between nearby buildings?

A. UTP

B. Coaxial

C. Fiber

D. Cat 5

E. Twinaxial

Answer(s): C

QUESTION: 133

Which of the following is the physical security mechanism that would MOST likely be used to enter a secure site?

A. A landing page

B. An access control vestibule

C. A smart locker

D. A firewall

Answer(s): B

Reference:
https://en.wikipedia.org/wiki/Mantrap_(access_control)

QUESTION: 134

Which of the following BEST describes a North-South traffic flow?

A. A public Internet user accessing a published web server

B. A database server communicating with another clustered database server

C. A Layer 3 switch advertising routes to a router

D. A management application connecting to managed devices

Answer(s): A

QUESTION: 135

A network switch was installed to provide connectivity to cameras monitoring wildlife in a remote location. The organization is concerned that intruders could potentially leverage unattended equipment in the remotelocation to connect rogue devices and gain access to the organization's resources. Which of the following techniques would BEST address the concern?

A. Configure port security using MAC filtering.

B. Manually register the cameras on the switch address table.

C. Activate PoE+ on the active switchports.

D. Disable Neighbor Discovery Protocol on the switch.

Answer(s): A

QUESTION: 136

A technician is documenting an application that is installed on a server and needs to verify all existing web and database connections to the server. Which of the following tools should the technician use to accomplish this task?

A. tracert

B. ipconfig

C. netstat

D. nslookup

Answer(s): C

QUESTION: 137

A technician is assisting a user who cannot access network resources when the workstation is connected to a VoIP phone. The technician identifies the phone as faulty and replaces it. According to troubleshooting methodology, which of the following should the technician do NEXT?

A. Implement the solution.

B. Test the theory.

C. Duplicate the issue.

D. Document the findings.

E. Verify functionality.

Answer(s): E

QUESTION: 138

Which of the following OSI model layers contains IP headers?

A. Presentation

B. Application

C. Data link

D. Network

E. Transport

Answer(s): D

QUESTION: 139

A small office is running WiFi 4 APs, and neighboring offices do not want to increase the throughput to associated devices. Which of the following is the MOST cost-efficient way for the office to increase network performance?

A. Add another AP.

B. Disable the 2.4GHz radios.

C. Enable channel bonding.

D. Upgrade to WiFi 5.

Answer(s): C

QUESTION: 140

A network technician is troubleshooting an application issue. The technician is able to recreate the issue in a virtual environment. According to the troubleshooting methodology, which of the following actions will the technician most likely perform NEXT?

A. Gather information from the initial report.

B. Escalate the issue to a supervisor.

C. Implement a solution to resolve the issue.

D. Establish a theory of probable cause.

Answer(s): D

QUESTION: 141

Which of the following types of datacenter architectures will MOST likely be used in a large SDN and can be extended beyond the datacenter? (Choose two.)

A. iSCSI

B. FCoE

C. Three-tiered network

D. Spine and leaf

E. Top-of-rack switching

Answer(s): C,D

QUESTION: 142

A technician is troubleshooting a client's report about poor wireless performance. Using a client monitor, the technician notes the following   information:

SSID	Signal (RSSI)	Channel
Corporate	−50	9
Corporate	−69	10
Corporate	−67	11
Corporate	−63	6

Which of the following is MOST likely the cause of the issue?

A. Channel overlap

B. Poor signal

C. Incorrect power settings

D. Wrong antenna type

Answer(s): A

QUESTION: 143

A network technician reviews an entry on the syslog server and discovers the following message from a switch:

SPANNING-TREE   Port   1/1   BLOCKED

Which of the following describes the issue?

A. A loop was discovered, and the impact was mitigated.

B. An incorrectly pinned cable was disconnected.

C. The link-local address on the port is incorrect.

D. The port was shut down, and it needs to be reactivated.

Answer(s): A

QUESTION: 144

A company just migrated its email service to a cloud solution. After the migration, two-thirds of the internal users were able to connect to their mailboxes, but the connection fails for the other one-third of internal users. Users working externally are not reporting any issues. The network administrator identifies the following output collected from an internal host:

c:\user>nslookup newmail.company.com Non-Authoritative answer: Name: newmail.company.com IPs: 3.219.13.186, 64.58.225.184, 184.168.131.243

Which of the following verification tasks should the network administrator perform NEXT?

A. Check the firewall ACL to verify all required IP addresses are included.

B. Verify the required router PAT rules are properly configured.

C. Confirm the internal DNS server is replying to requests for the cloud solution.

D. Validate the cloud console to determine whether there are unlicensed requests.

Answer(s): A

QUESTION: 145

A network technician was hired to harden the security of a network. The technician is required to enable encryption and create a password for AP security through the web browser. Which of the following would BEST support these requirements?

A. ESP

B. WPA2

C. IPSec

D. ACL

Answer(s): B

QUESTION: 146

Which of the following ports are associated with IMAP? (Choose two.)

A. 25

B. 110

C. 143

D. 587

E. 993

F. 995

Answer(s): C,E

Reference:
https://billing.precedence.com.au/billing/knowledgebase/70/Mail-Ports-for-POP3-IMAP-and-SMTP.html

QUESTION: 147

A network administrator is trying to identify a device that is having issues connecting to a switchport. Which of the following would BEST help identify the issue?

A. A syslog server

B. Change management records

C. A rack diagram

D. The security log

Answer(s): A

QUESTION: 148

A company with multiple routers would like to implement an HA network gateway with the least amount of downtime possible. This solution should not require changes on the gateway setting of the network clients. Which of the following should a technician configure?

A. Automate a continuous backup and restore process of the system's state of the active gateway.

B. Use a static assignment of the gateway IP address on the network clients.

C. Configure DHCP relay and allow clients to receive a new IP setting.

D. Configure a shared VIP and deploy VRRP on the routers.

Answer(s): D

QUESTION: 149

Which of the following protocols would allow a secure connection to a Linux-based system?

A. SMB

B. FTP

C. RDP

D. SSH

Answer(s): D

QUESTION: 150

A network administrator is troubleshooting the communication between two Layer 2 switches that are reporting a very high runt count. After trying multiple ports on both switches, the issue persists. Which of the following should the network administrator perform to resolve the issue?

A. Increase the MTU size on both switches.

B. Recertify the cable between both switches.

C. Perform a factory reset on both switches.

D. Enable debug logging on both switches.

Answer(s): B

QUESTION: 151

Users attending security training at work are advised not to use single words as passwords for corporate applications. Which of the following does this BEST protect against?

A. An on-path attack

B. A brute-force attack

C. A dictionary attack

D. MAC spoofing

E. Denial of service

Answer(s): C

QUESTION: 152

A network administrator would like to enable NetFlow on a Layer 3 switch but is concerned about how the feature may impact the switch. Which of the following metrics should the administrator graph using SNMP to BEST measure the feature's impact?

A. CPU usage

B. Temperature

C. Electrical consumption

D. Bandwidth usage

Answer(s): A

Reference:

QUESTION: 153

Which of the following would be used to enforce and schedule critical updates with supervisory approval and include backup plans in case of failure?

A. Business continuity plan

B. Onboarding and offboarding policies

C. Acceptable use policy

D. System life cycle

E. Change management

Answer(s): E

QUESTION: 154

A newly installed VoIP phone is not getting the DHCP IP address it needs to connect to the phone system. Which of the following tasks need to be completed to allow the phone to operate correctly?

A. Assign the phone's switchport to the correct VLAN

B. Statistically assign the phone's gateway address

C. Configure a route on the VoIP network router

D. Implement a VoIP gateway

Answer(s): A

QUESTION: 155

Users are reporting intermittent WiFi connectivity in a specific parts of a building. Which of the following should the network administrator check FIRST when troubleshooting this issue? (Choose two.)

A. Site survey

B. EIRP

C. AP placement

D. Captive portal

E. SSID assignment

F. AP association time

Answer(s): A,C

A technician is setting up a new router, configuring ports, and allowing access to the Internet. However, none of the users connected to this new router are able to connect to the Internet. Which of the following does the technician need to configure?

A. Tunneling

B. Multicast routing

C. Network address translation

D. Router advertisement

Answer(s): C

A network administrator is testing performance improvements by configuring channel bonding on an 802.11ac AP. Although a site survey detected the majority of the 5GHz frequency spectrum was idle, being used only by the company's WLAN and a nearby government radio system, the AP is not allowing the administrator to manually configure a large portion of the 5GHz frequency range.

Which of the following would be BEST to configure for the WLAN being tested?

A. Upgrade the equipment to an AP that supports manual configuration of the EIRP power settings

B. Switch to 802.11n, disable channel auto-selection, and enforce channel bonding on configuration

C. Set up the AP to perform a dynamic selection of the frequency according to regulatory requirements

D. Deactivate the band 5GHz to avoid interference with the government radio

Answer(s): C

QUESTION: 158

Which of the following options represents the participating computers in a network?

A. Nodes

B. CPUs

C. Servers

D. Clients

Answer(s): A

QUESTION: 159

An administrator is working with the local ISP to troubleshoot an issue. Which of the following should the ISP use to define the furthest point on the network that the administrator is responsible for troubleshooting?

A. Firewall

B. A CSU/DSU

C. Demarcation point

D. Router

E. Patch panel

Answer(s): D

QUESTION: 160

To access production applications and data, developers must first connect remotely to a different server. From there, the developers are able to access production data. Which of the following does this BEST represent?

A. A management plane

B. A proxy server

C. An out-of-band management device

D. A site-to-site VPN

E. A jump box

Answer(s): E

QUESTION: 161

Which of the following is conducted frequently to maintain an updated list of a system's weaknesses?

A. Penetration test

B. Posture assessment

C. Risk assessment

D. Vulnerability scan

Answer(s): D

QUESTION: 162

A systems administrator wants to use the least amount of equipment to segment two departments that have cables terminating in the same room. Which of the following would allow this to occur?

A. Load balancer

B. Proxy server

C. A Layer 3 switch

D. Hub

E. A Layer 7 firewall

Answer(s): C

QUESTION: 163

An administrator needs to connect two laptops directly to each other using 802. 11ac but does not have an AP available. Which of the following describes this configuration?

A. Basic service set

B. Extended service set

C. Independent basic service set

D. MU-MIMO

Answer(s): C

QUESTION: 164

A network administrator is reviewing the following metrics from a network management system regarding a switchport. The administrator suspects an issue because users are calling in regards to the switch port's performance:

Metric	Value
Uptime	201 days, 3 hours, 18 minutes
MDIX	On
CRCs	0
Giants	2508
Output queue maximum	40
Packets input	136208849
Packets output	64458087024

Based on the information in the chart above, which of the following is
the cause of these performance issues?

A. The connected device is exceeding the configured MTU.

B. The connected device is sending too many packets.

C. The switchport has been up for too long.

D. The connected device is receiving too many packets.

E. The switchport does not have enough CRCs.

Answer(s): A

A network administrator is installing a new server in the datacenter. The administrator is concerned the amount of traffic generated will exceed 1GB, and higher- throughput NICs are not available for installation. Which of the following is the BEST solution for this issue?

A. Install an additional NIC and configure LACP

B. Remove some of the applications from the server

C. Configure the NIC to use full duplex

D. Configure port mirroring to send traffic to another server

E. Install a SSD to decrease data processing time

Answer(s): A

A malicious user is using special software to perform an on-path attack. Which of the following best practices should be configured to mitigate this threat?

A. Dynamic ARP inspection

B. Role-based access

C. Control plane policing

D. MAC filtering

Answer(s): A

QUESTION: 167

Which of the following can be used to store various types of devices and provide contactless delivery to users?

A. Asset tags

B. Biometrics

C. Access control vestibules

D. Smart lockers

Answer(s): D

QUESTION: 168

A technician recently set up a small office network for nine users. When the installation was complete, all the computers on the network showed addresses ranging from 169.254.0.0 to 169.254.255.255. Which of the following types of address ranges does this represent?

A. Private

B. Public

C. APIPA

D. Classless

Answer(s): C

QUESTION: 170

A network technician at a university is assisting with the planning of a simultaneous software deployment to multiple computers in one classroom in a building. Which of the following would be BEST to use?

A. Multicast

B. Anycast

C. Unicast

D. Broadcast

Answer(s): A

QUESTION: 171

Which of the following describes the BEST device to configure as a DHCP relay?

A. Bridge

B. Router

C. Layer 2 switch

D. Hub

Answer(s): B

QUESTION: 172

Which of the following compromises Internet-connected devices and makes them vulnerable to becoming part of a botnet? (Choose two.)

A. Deauthentication attack

B. Malware infection

C. IP spoofing

D. Firmware corruption

E. Use of default credentials

F. Dictionary attack

Answer(s): B,E

QUESTION: 173

A network administrator is planning a WLAN for a soccer stadium and was advised to use MU-MIMO to improve connection performance in high-density areas. The project requires compatibility with clients connecting using 2.4GHz or 5GHz frequencies. Which of the following would be the BEST wireless standard for this project?

A. 802.11ac

B. 802.11ax

C. 802.11g

D. 802.11n

Answer(s): B

An organization purchased an allocation of public IPv4 addresses. Instead of receiving the network address and subnet mask, the purchase paperwork indicates the allocation is a /28. This type of notation is referred to as:

A. CIDR

B. classful

C. classless

D. RFC1918

Answer(s): A

A network technician is reviewing a document that specifies how to handle access to company resources, such as the Internet and printers, when devices are not part of the company's assets. Which of the following agreements would a user be required to accept before using the company's resources?

A. BYOD

B. DLP

C. AUP

D. MOU

Answer(s): C

QUESTION: 176

Which of the following records can be used to track the number of changes on a DNS zone?

A. SOA

B. SRV

C. TXT

D. NS

Answer(s): A

QUESTION: 177

A network administrator is trying to add network redundancy for the server farm. Which of the following can the network administrator configure to BEST provide this capability?

A. VRRP

B. DNS

C. UPS

D. RPO

Answer(s): A

QUESTION: 178

A network administrator is adding a new switch to the network. Which of the following network hardening techniques would be BEST to use once the switch is in production?

A. Disable unneeded ports

B. Disable SSH service

C. Disable MAC filtering

D. Disable port security

Answer(s): A

QUESTION: 179

A network administrator is troubleshooting an issue with a new Internet connection. The ISP is asking detailed questions about the configuration of the router that the network administrator is troubleshooting. Which of the following commands is the network administrator using? (Choose two.)

A. tcpdump

B. show config

C. hostname

D. show route

E. netstat

F. show ip arp

Answer(s): B,D

QUESTION: 180

Which of the following is the MOST appropriate use case for the deployment of a clientless VPN?

A. Secure web access to internal corporate resources.

B. Upgrade security via the use of an NFV technology.

C. Connect two datacenters across the Internet.

D. Increase VPN availability by using a SDWAN technology.

Answer(s): A

QUESTION: 182

A network technician needs to install security updates on several switches on the company's network. The management team wants this completed as quickly and efficiently as possible. Which of the following should the technician do to perform the updates?

A. Upload the security update onto each switch using a terminal emulator and a console cable.

B. Configure a TFTP server, SSH into each device, and perform the update.

C. Replace each old switch with new switches that have the updates already performed.

D. Connect a USB memory stick to each switch and perform the update.

Answer(s): B

Which of the following describes traffic going in and out of a data center from the internet?

A. Demarcation point

B. North-South

C. Fibre Channel

D. Spine and leaf

Answer(s): B

A technician is troubleshooting a connectivity issue with an end user. The end user can access local network shares and intranet pages but is unable to access the internet or remote resources. Which of the following needs to be reconfigured?

A. The IP address

B. The subnet mask

C. The gateway address

D. The DNS servers

Answer(s): C

QUESTION: 185

An IT administrator received an assignment with the following objectives:
-Conduct a total scan within the company's network for all connected hosts.
-Detect all the types of operating systems running on all devices.
-Discover all services offered by hosts on the network.
-Find open ports and detect security risks.

Which of the following command-line tools can be used to achieve these objectives?

A. nmap

B. arp

C. netstat

D. tcpdump

Answer(s): A

QUESTION: 186

A network manager is configuring switches in IDFs to ensure unauthorized client computers are not connecting to a secure wired network. Which of the following is the network manager MOST likely performing?

A. Disabling unneeded switchports

B. Changing the default VLAN

C. Configuring DHCP snooping

D. Writing ACLs to prevent access to the switch

Answer(s): A

QUESTION: 187

At which of the following OSI model layers does routing occur?

A. Data link

B. Transport

C. Physical

D. Network

Answer(s): D

QUESTION: 188

An auditor assessing network best practices was able to connect a rogue switch into a network jack and get network connectivity. Which of the following controls would BEST address this risk?

A. Activate port security on the switchports providing end user access.

B. Deactivate Spanning Tree Protocol on network interfaces that are facing public areas.

C. Disable Neighbor Resolution Protocol in the Layer 2 devices.

D. Ensure port tagging is in place for network interfaces in guest areas.

Answer(s): A

QUESTION: 189

A technician knows the MAC address of a device and is attempting to find the device's IP address. Which of the following should the technician look at to find the IP address? (Choose two.)

A. ARP table

B. DHCP leases

C. IP route table

D. DNS cache

E. MAC address table

F. STP topology

Answer(s): A,B

QUESTION: 190

A user in a branch office reports that access to all files has been lost after receiving a new PC. All other users in the branch can access fileshares. The IT engineer who is troubleshooting this incident is able to ping the workstation from the branch router, but the machine cannot, ping the router. Which of the following is MOST likely the cause of the incident?

A. Incorrect subnet mask

B. Incorrect DNS server

C. Incorrect IP class

D. Incorrect TCP port

Answer(s): A

QUESTION: 191

A network administrator would like to purchase a device that provides access ports to endpoints and has the ability to route between networks.
Which of the following would be BEST for the administrator to purchase?

A. An IPS

B. A Layer 3 switch

C. A router

D. A wireless LAN controller

Answer(s): B

QUESTION: 192

A false camera is installed outside a building to assist with physical security. Which of the following is the device assisting?

A. Detection

B. Recovery

C. Identification

D. Prevention

Answer(s): D

QUESTION: 193

Which of the following types of attacks can be used to gain credentials by setting up rogue APs with identical corporate SSIDs?

A. VLAN hopping

B. Evil twin

C. DNS poisoning

D. Social engineering

Answer(s): B

QUESTION: 194

Which of the following protocols is widely used in large-scale enterprise networks to support complex networks with multiple routers and balance traffic load on multiple links?

A. OSPF

B. RIPv2

C. QoS

D. STP

Answer(s): A

QUESTION: 195

A network engineer is investigating reports of poor network performance. Upon reviewing a report, the engineer finds hundreds of CRC errors on an interface. Which of the following is the MOST likely cause of these errors?

A. A bad wire on the Cat 5e cable

B. The wrong VLAN assignment to the switchport

C. A misconfigured QoS setting on the router

D. Both sides of the switch trunk set to full duplex

Answer(s): A

Which of the following is considered a physical security detection device?

A. Cameras

B. Biometric readers

C. Access control vestibules

D. Locking racks

Answer(s): A

A network is experiencing extreme latency when accessing a particular website. Which of the following commands will BEST help identify the issue?

A. ipconfig

B. netstat

C. tracert

D. ping

Answer(s): C

QUESTION: 198

A technician needs to configure a routing protocol for an internet-facing edge router. Which of the following routing protocols will the technician MOST likely use?

A. BGP

B. RIPv2

C. OSPF

D. EIGRP

Answer(s): A

QUESTION: 199

A technician is monitoring a network interface and notices the device is dropping packets. The cable and interfaces, however, are in working order. Which of the following is MOST likely the cause?

A. OID duplication

B. MIB mismatch

C. CPU usage

D. Encapsulation errors

Answer(s): C

QUESTION: 200

A technician installed an 8-port switch in a user's office. The user needs to add a second computer in the office, so the technician connects both PCs to the switch and connects the switch to the wall jack. However, the new PC cannot connect to network resources. The technician   then   observes   the   following:
-The new computer does not get an IP address on the client's VLAN.
-Both   computers   have   a   link   light   on   their   NICs.
-The new PC appears to be operating normally except for the network issue.
-The   existing   computer   operates   normally.

Which of the following should the technician do NEXT to address the situation?

A. Contact the network team to resolve the port security issue.

B. Contact the server team to have a record created in DNS for the new PC.

C. Contact the security team to review the logs on the company's SIEM.

D. Contact the application team to check NetFlow data from the connected switch.

Answer(s): A

www.ingramcontent.com/pod-product-compliance
Lightning Source LLC
La Vergne TN
LVHW051657050326
832903LV00032B/3859